Calm your mind and spare few hours to relax and enjoy.

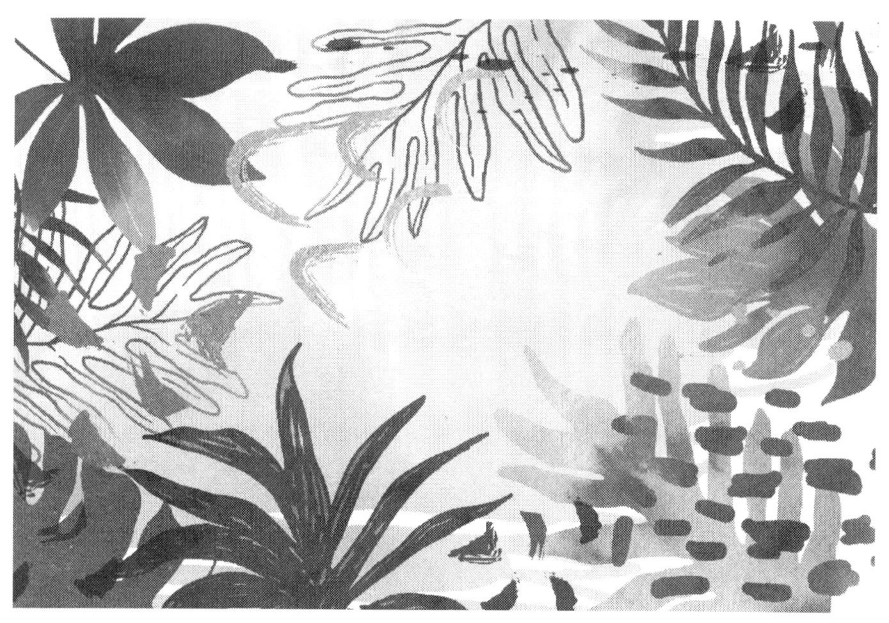

About You:

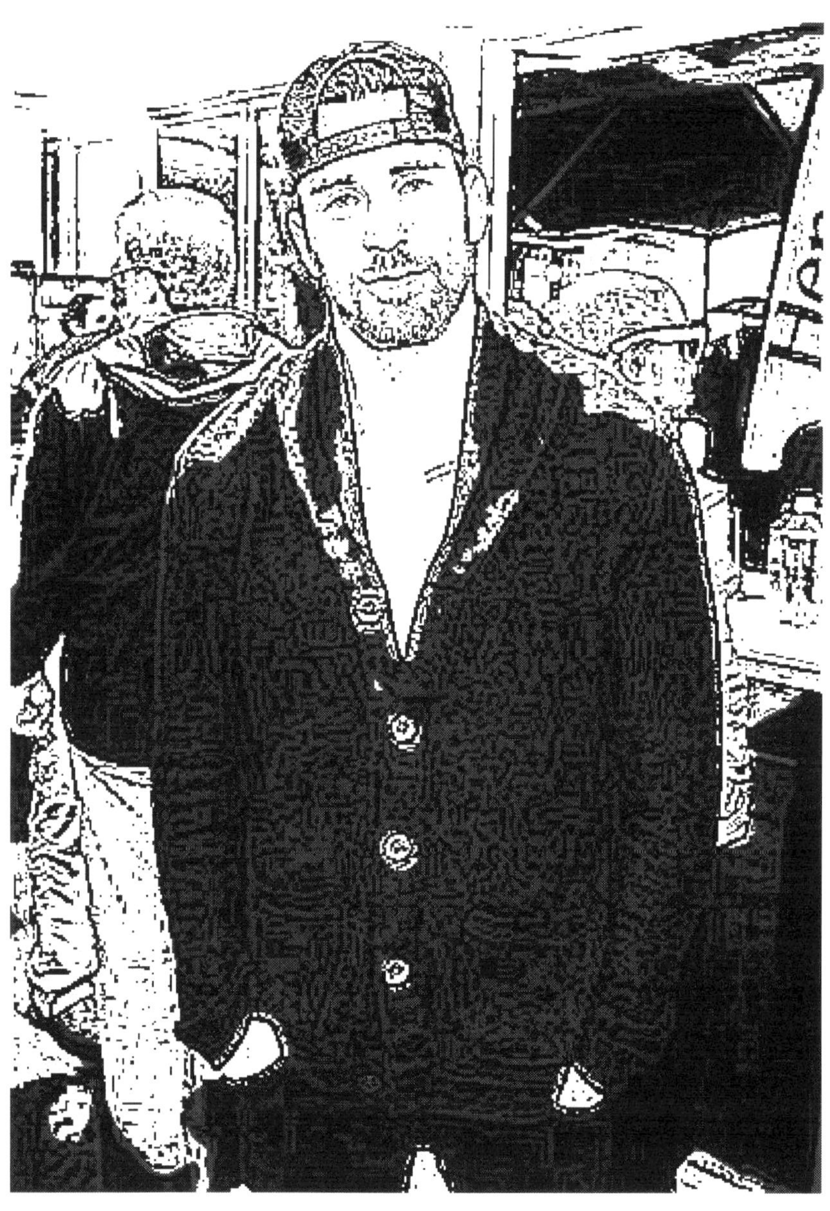

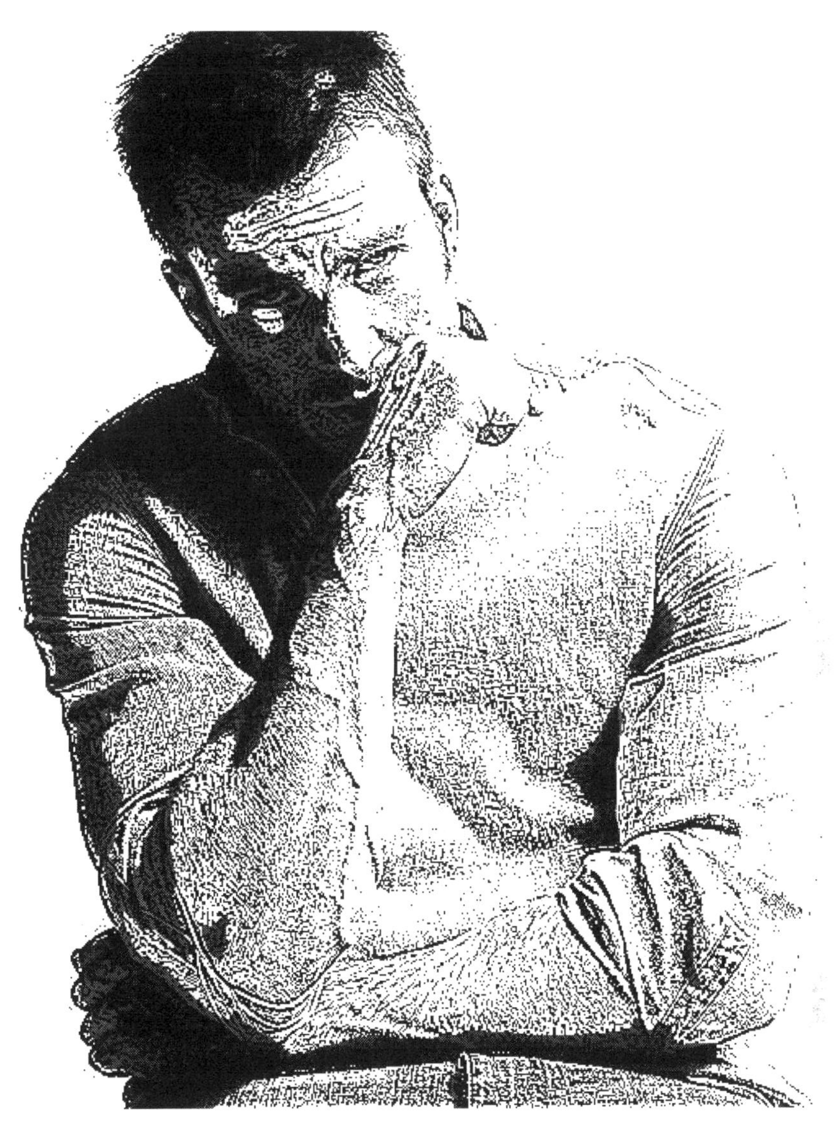

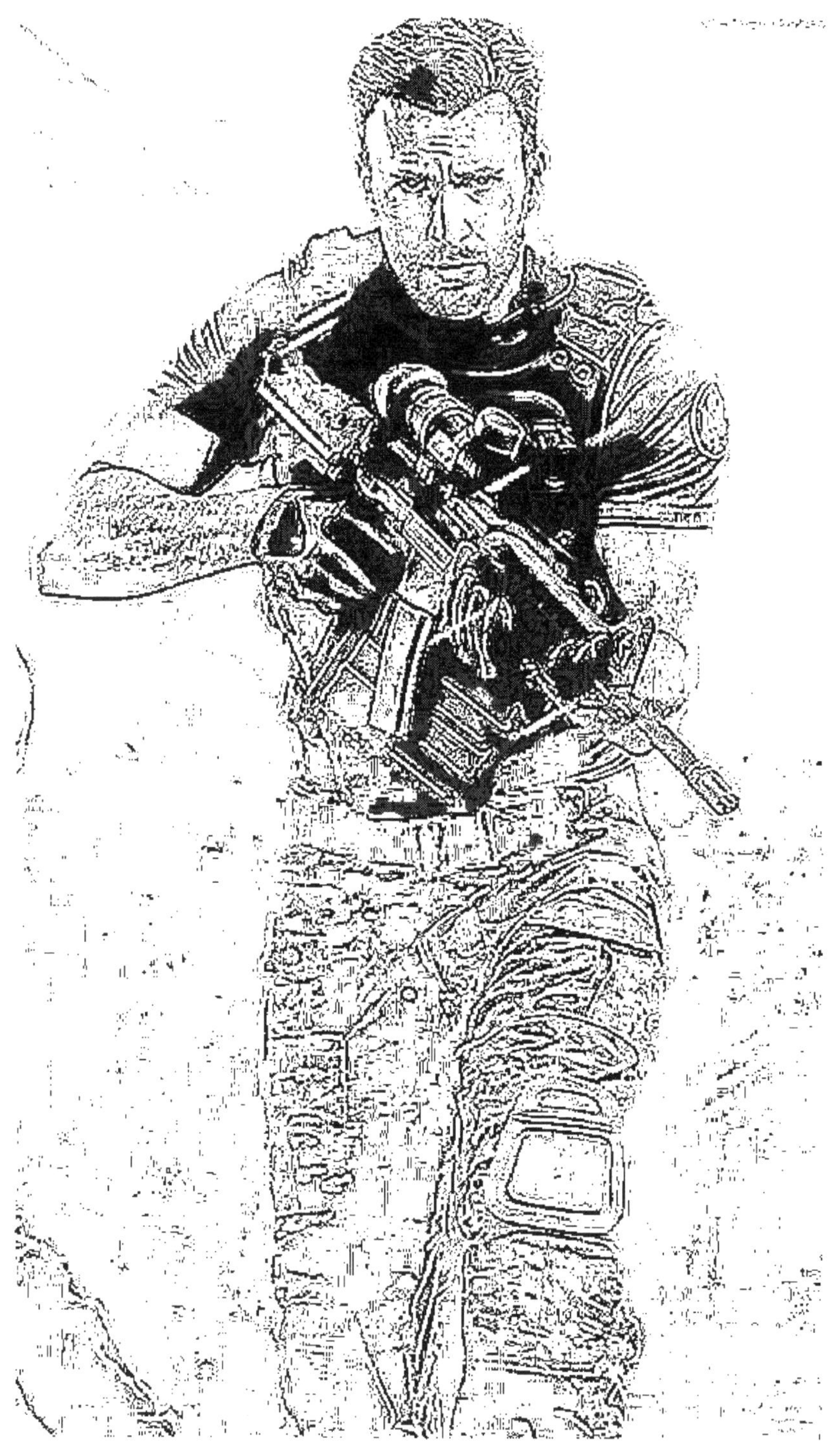

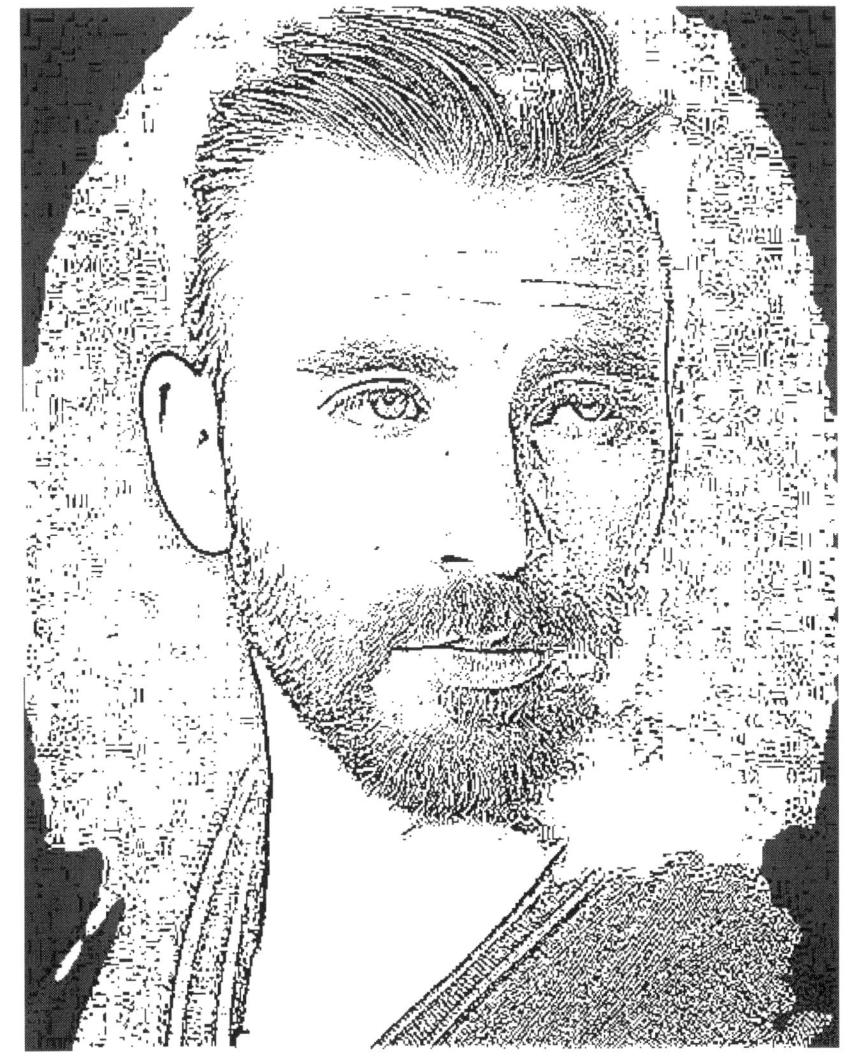

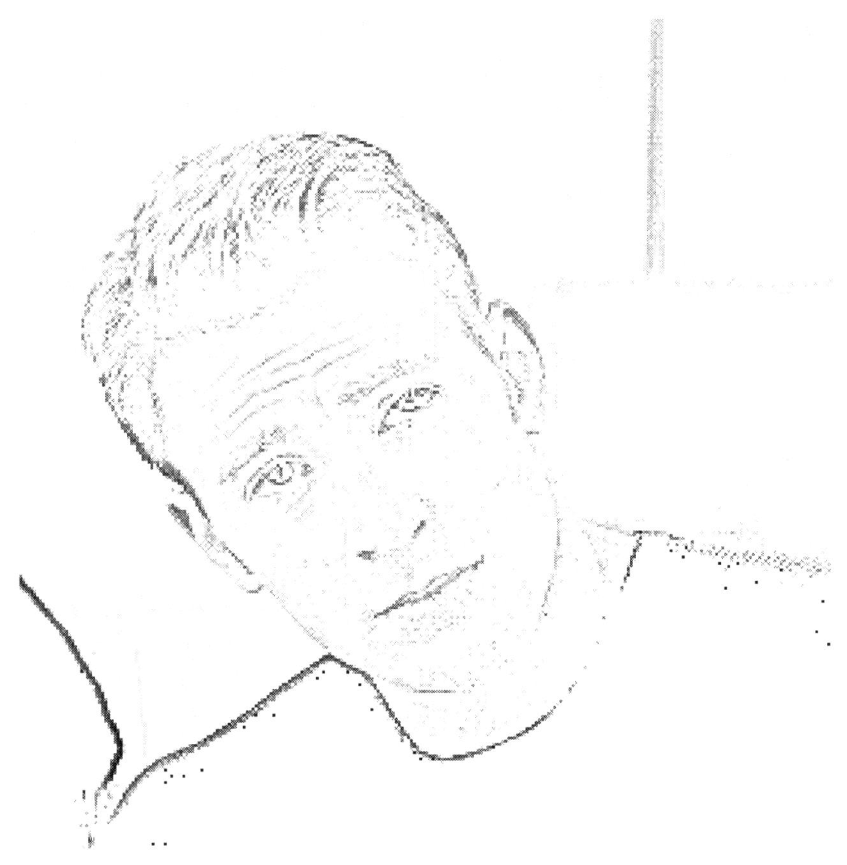

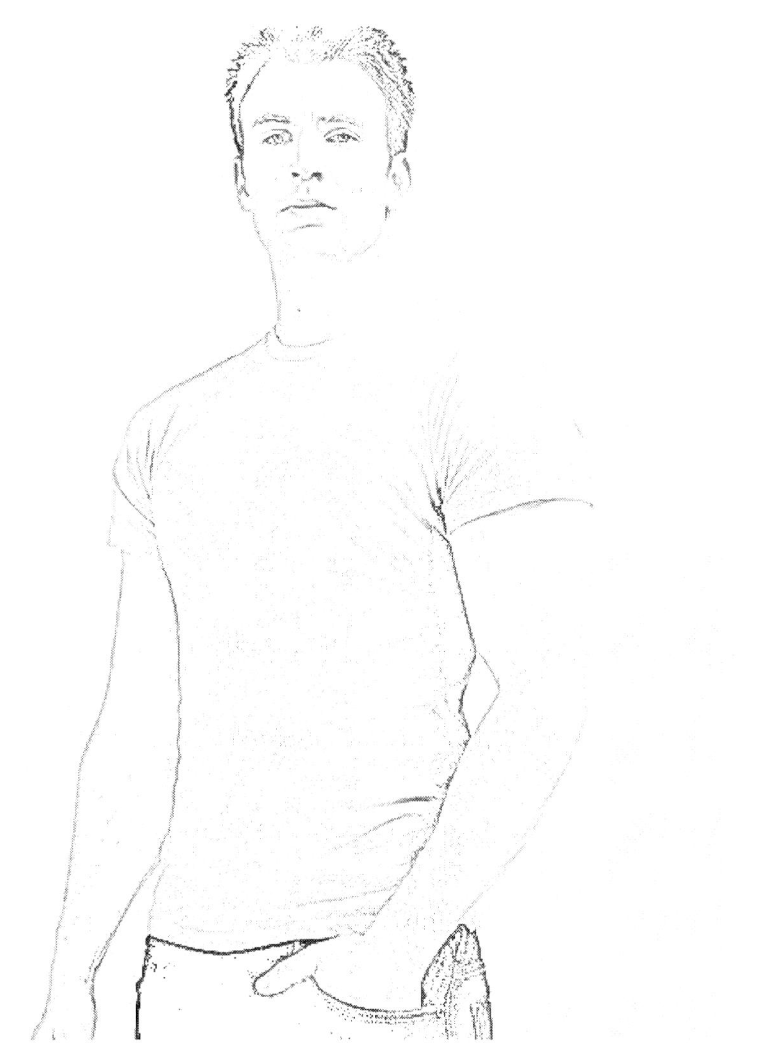

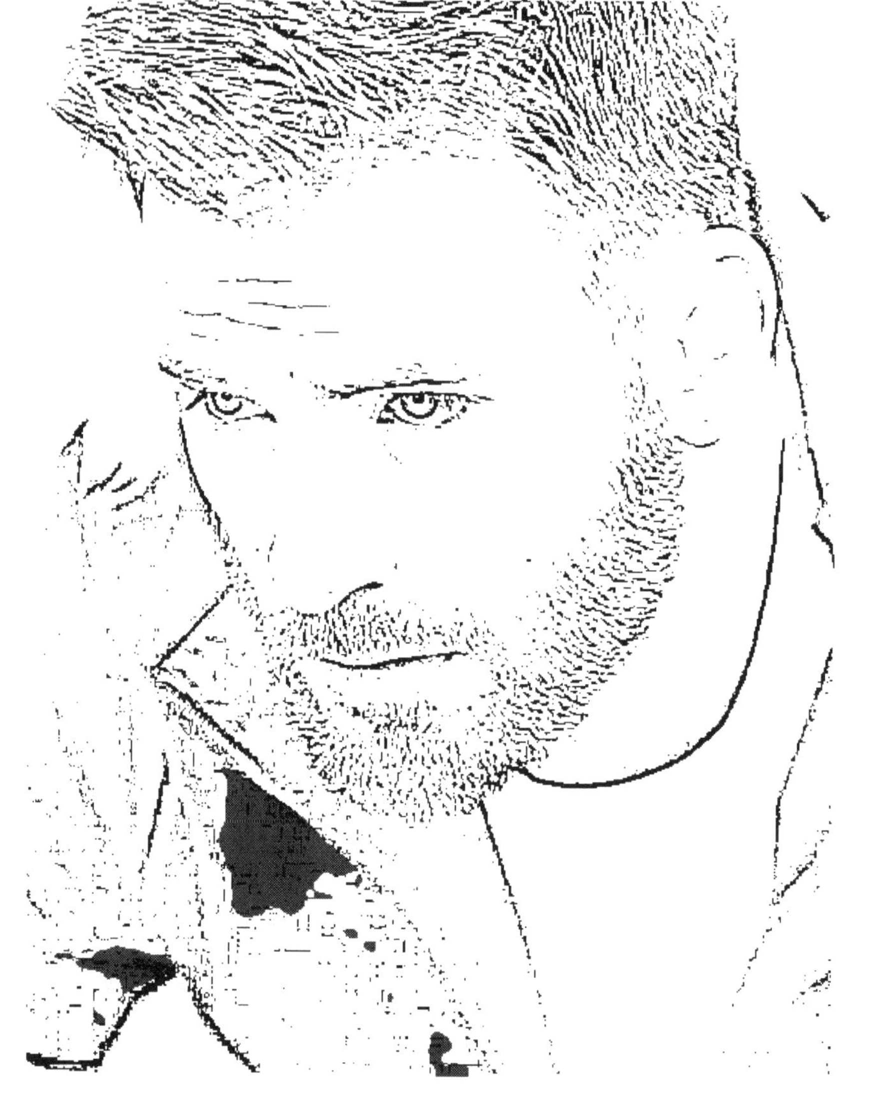

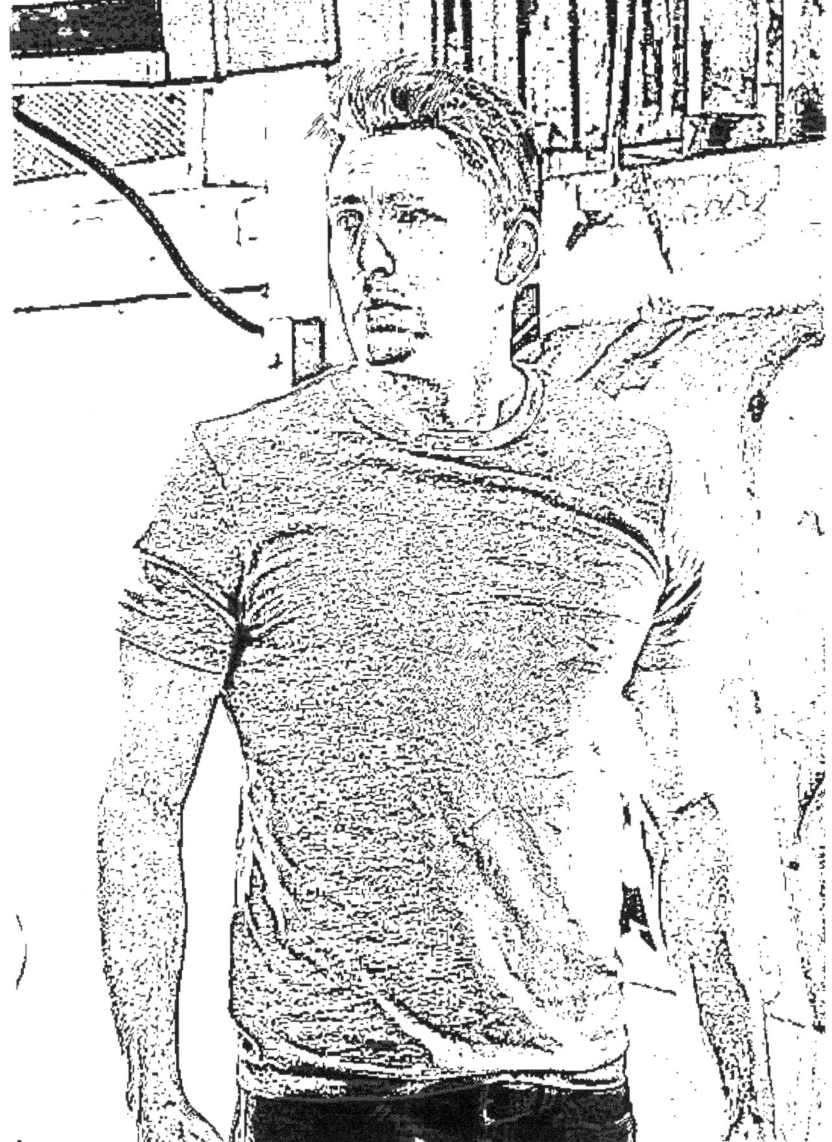

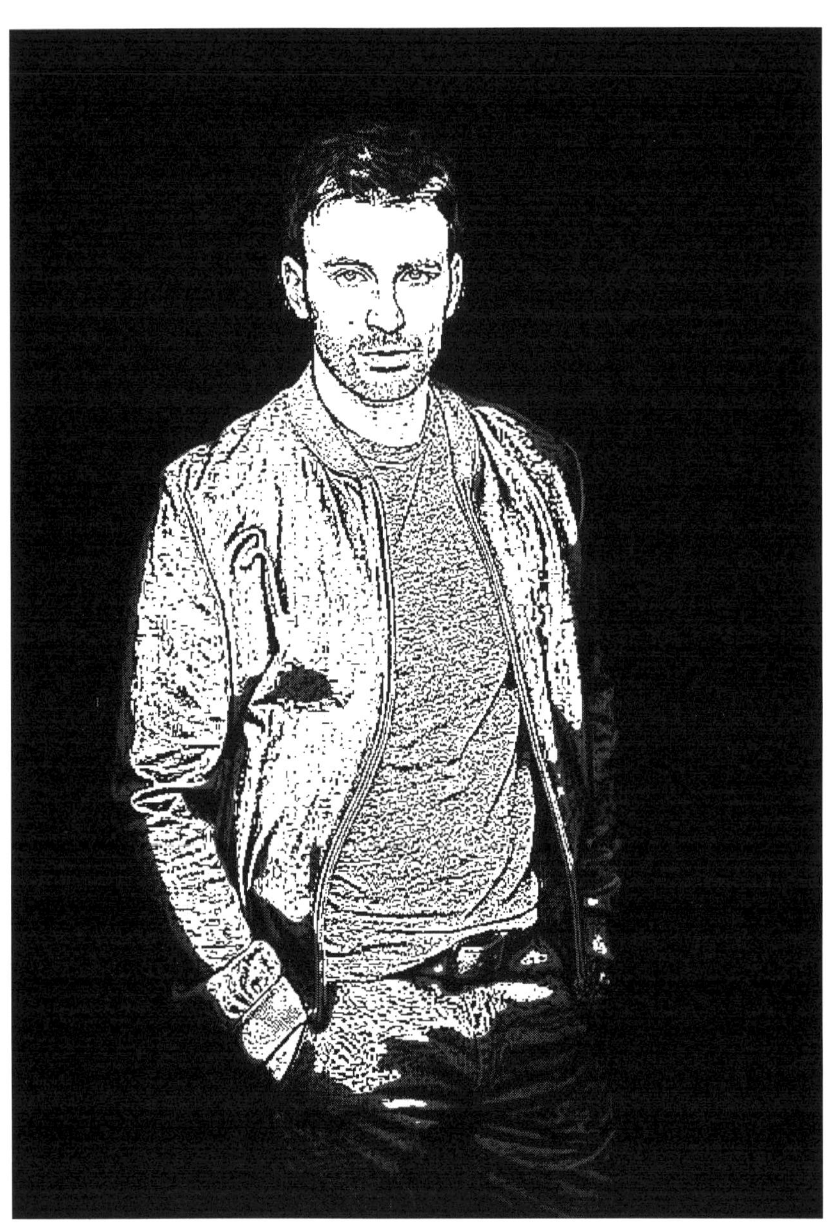

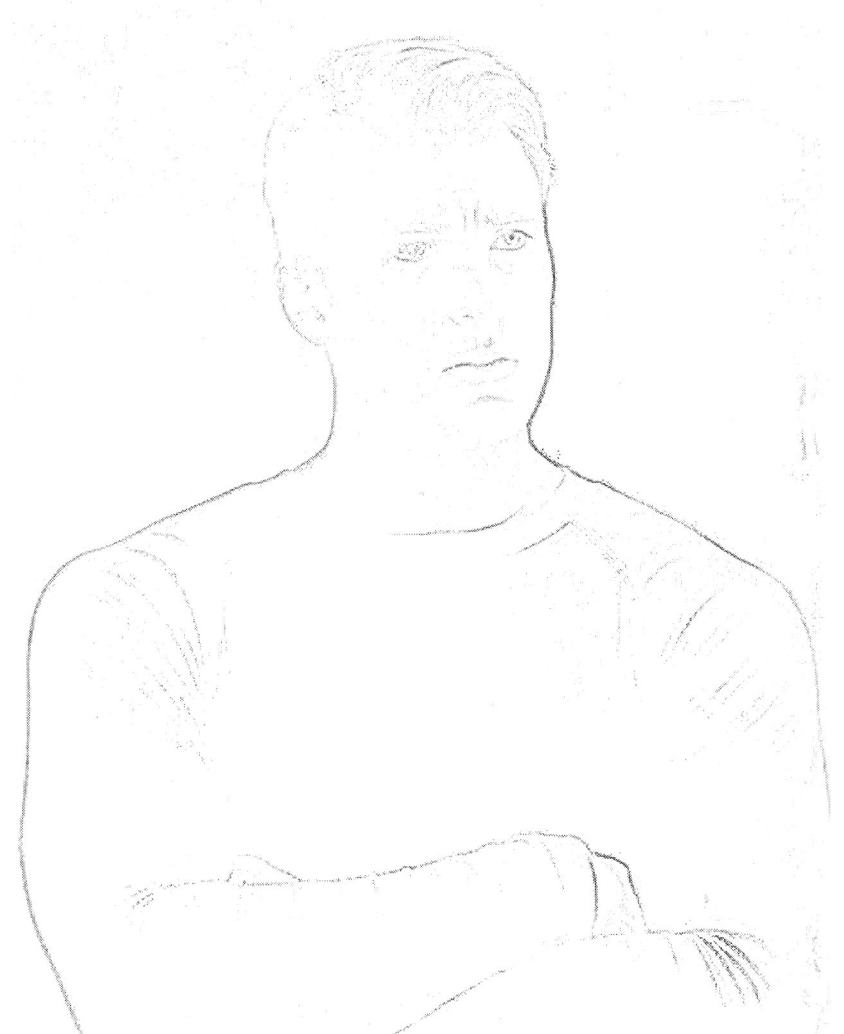

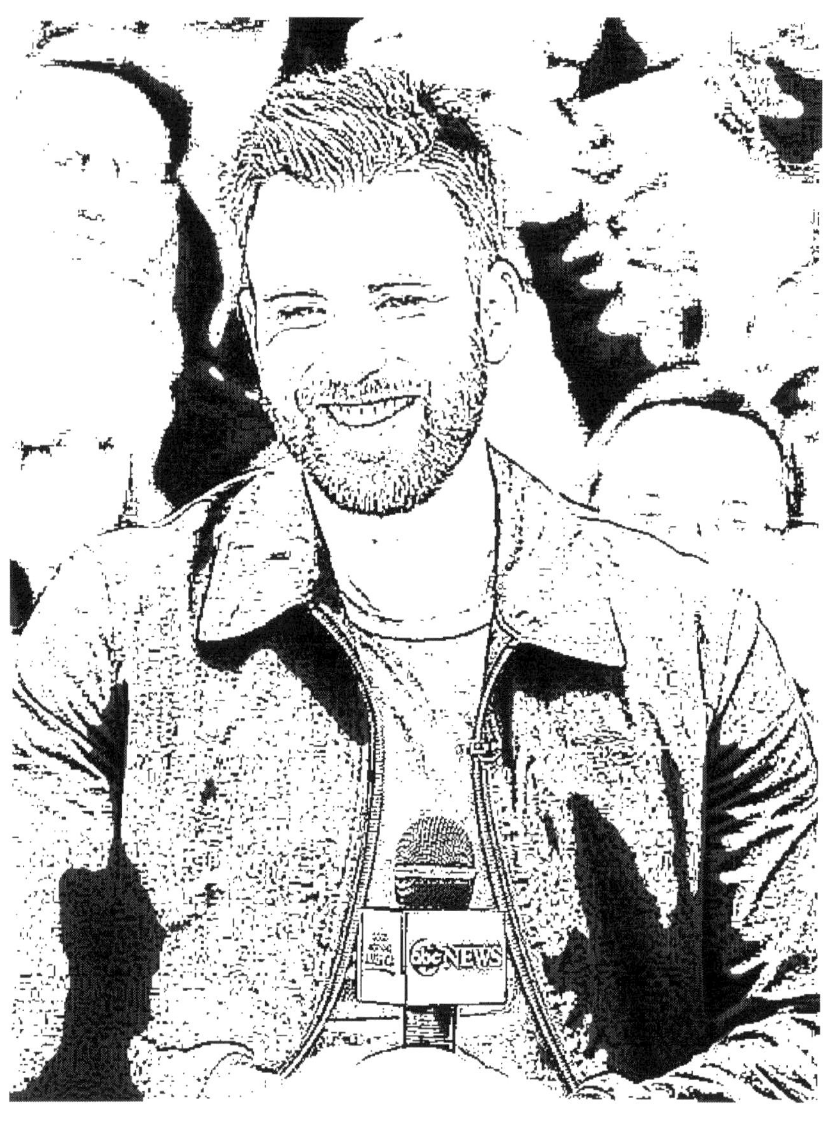
abcNEWS

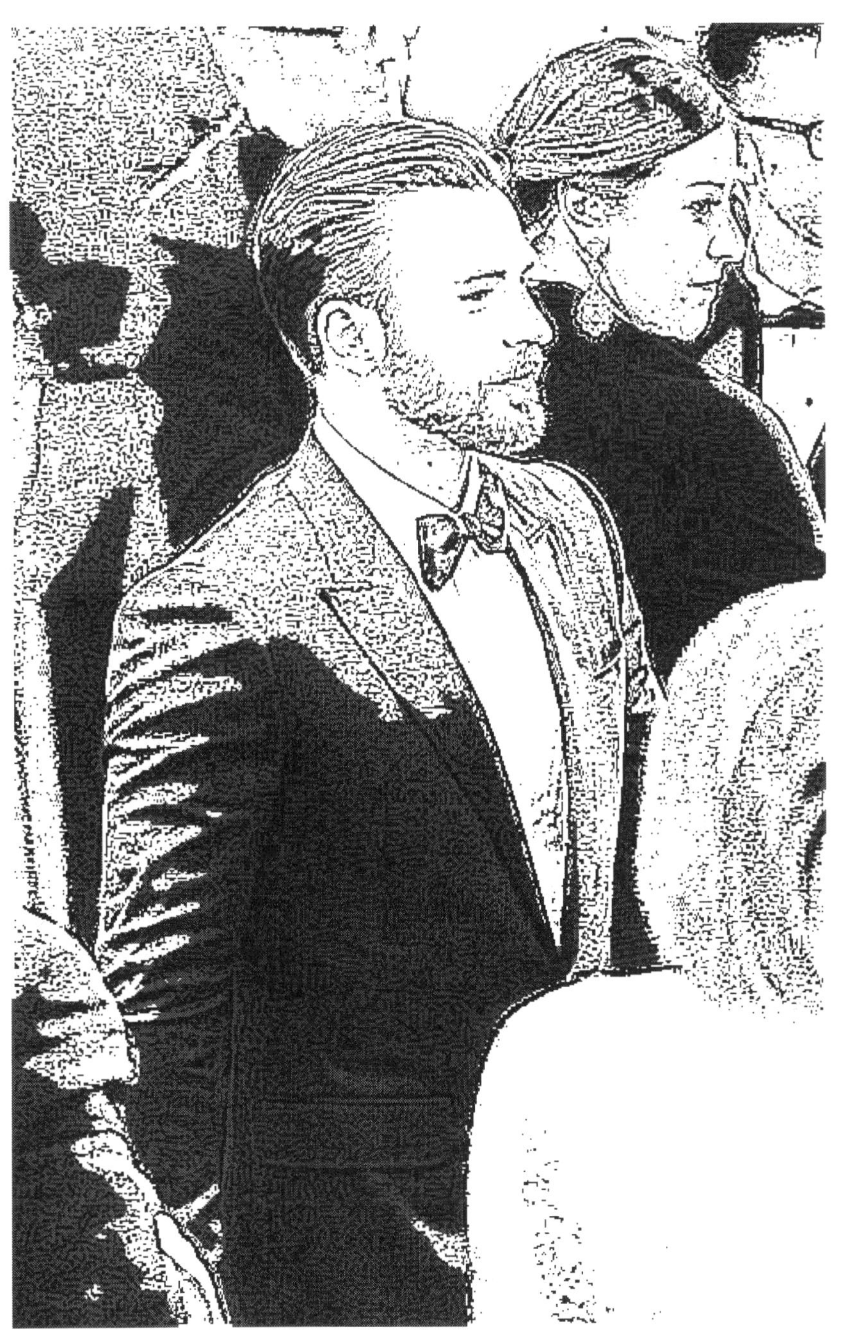

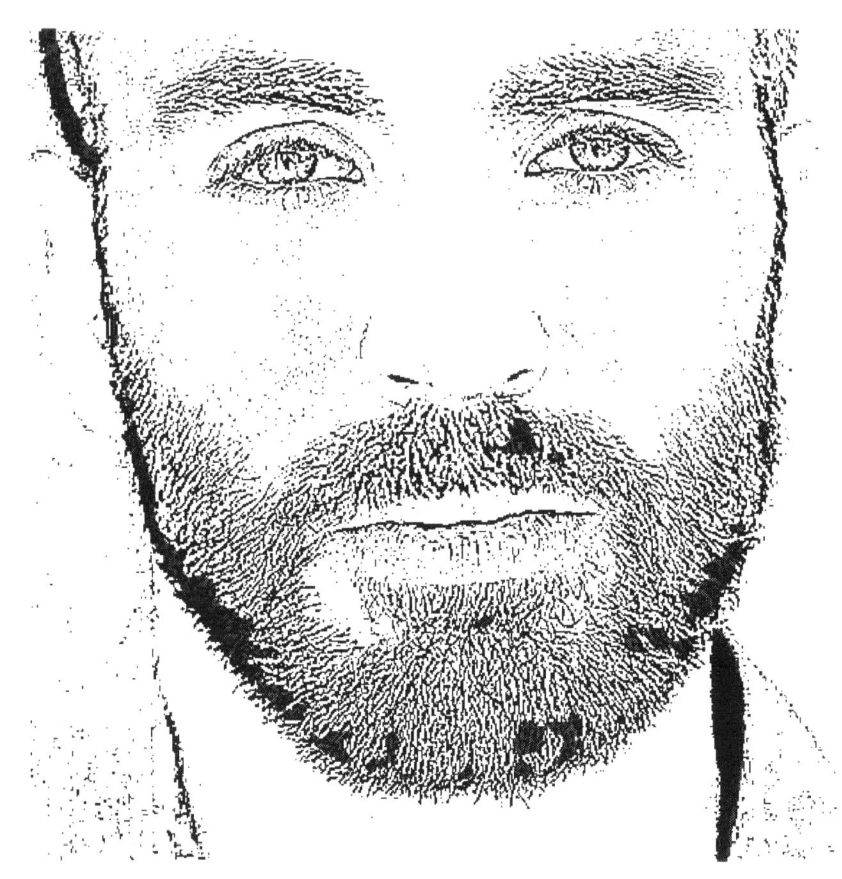

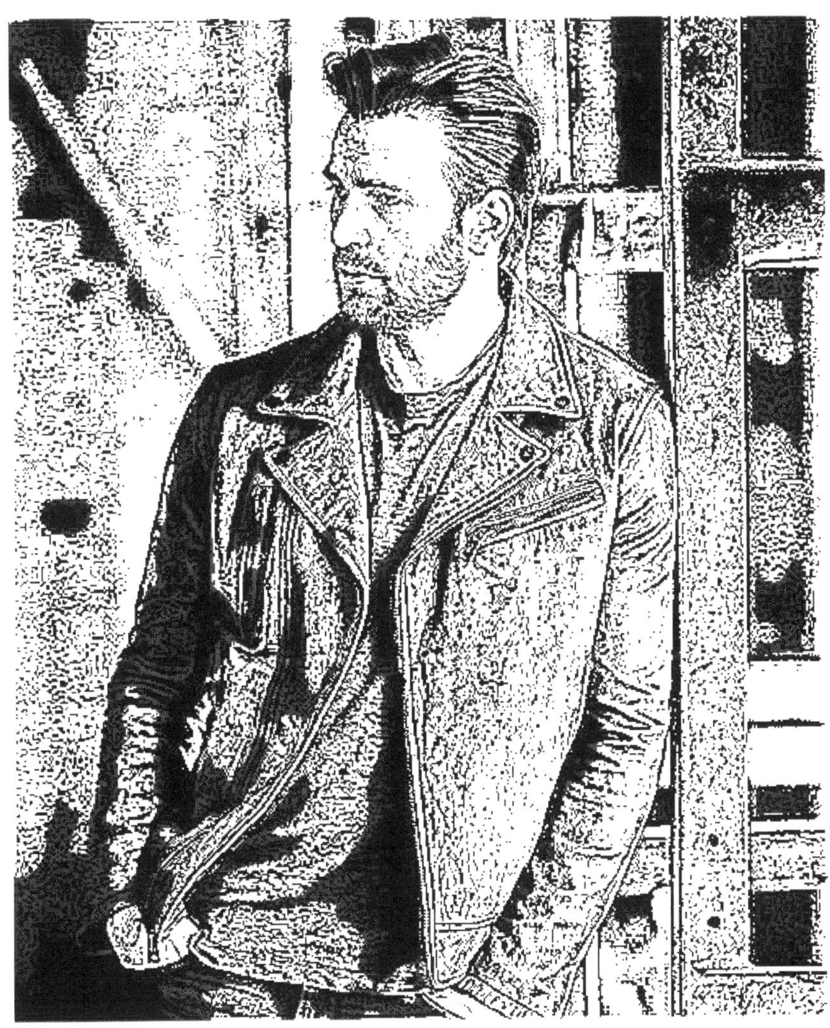

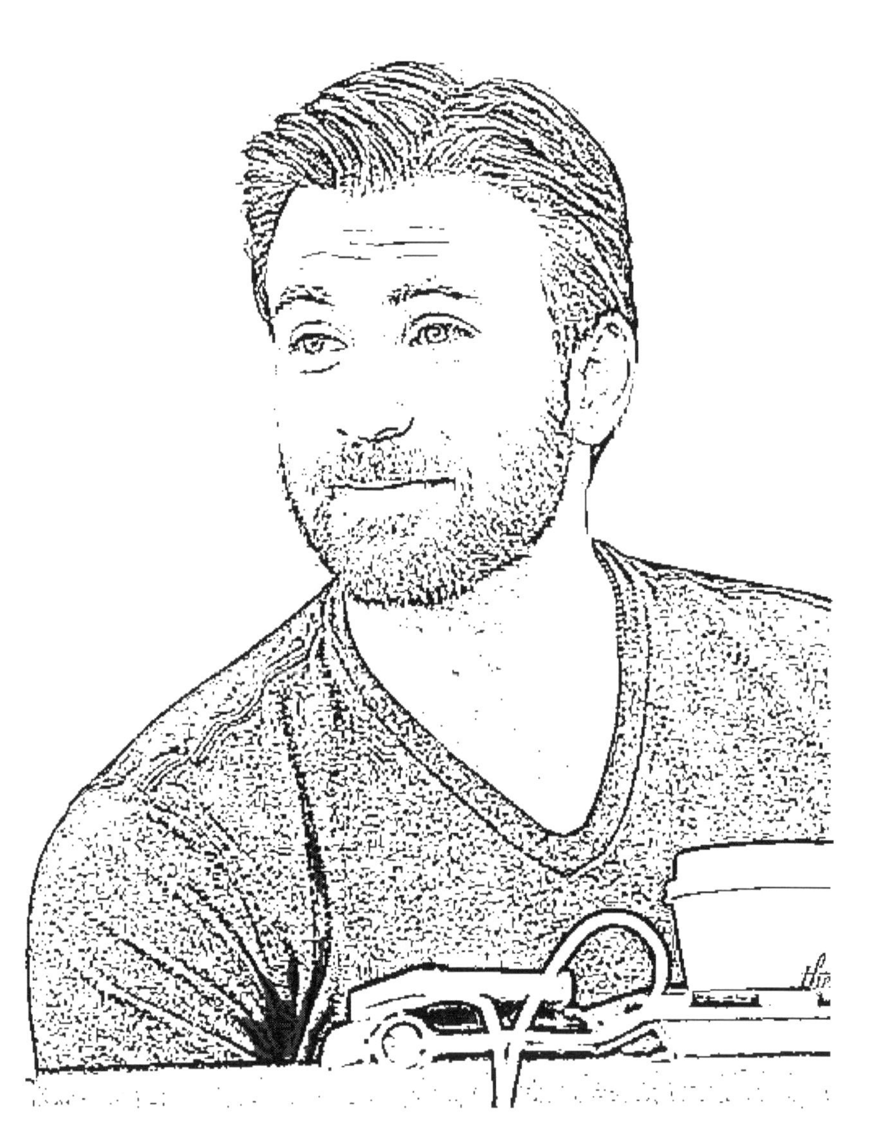

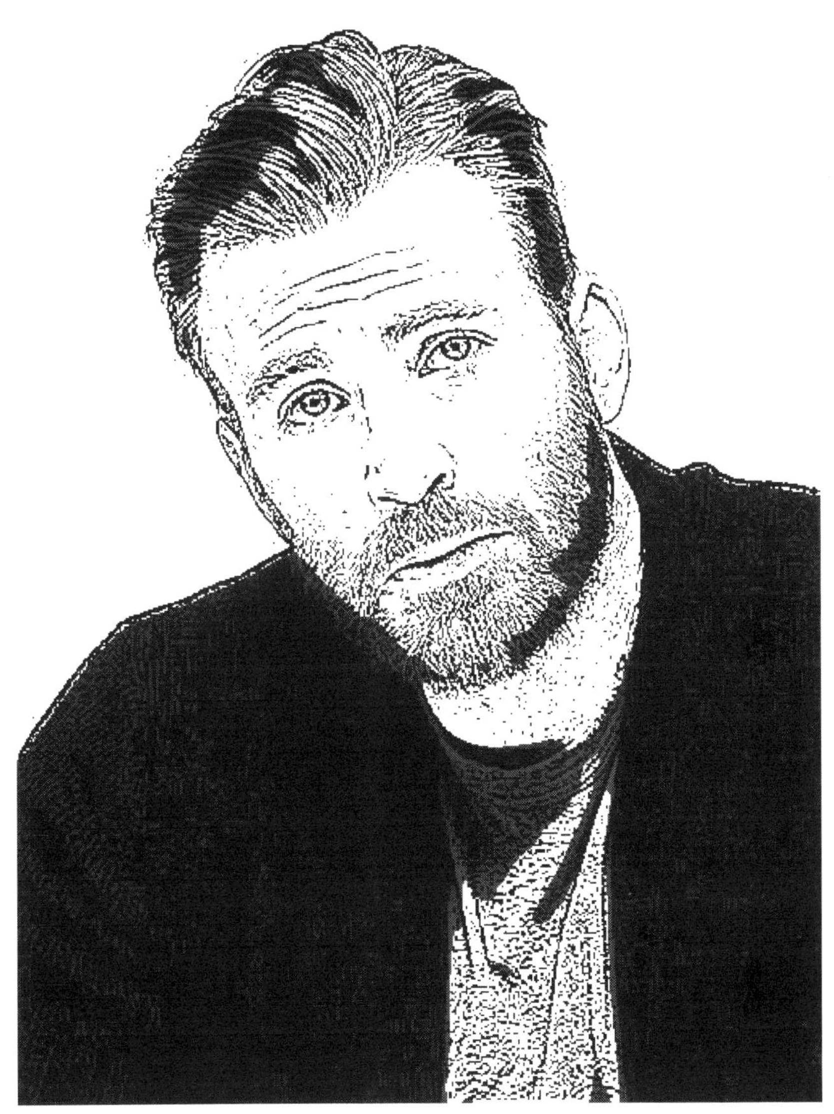

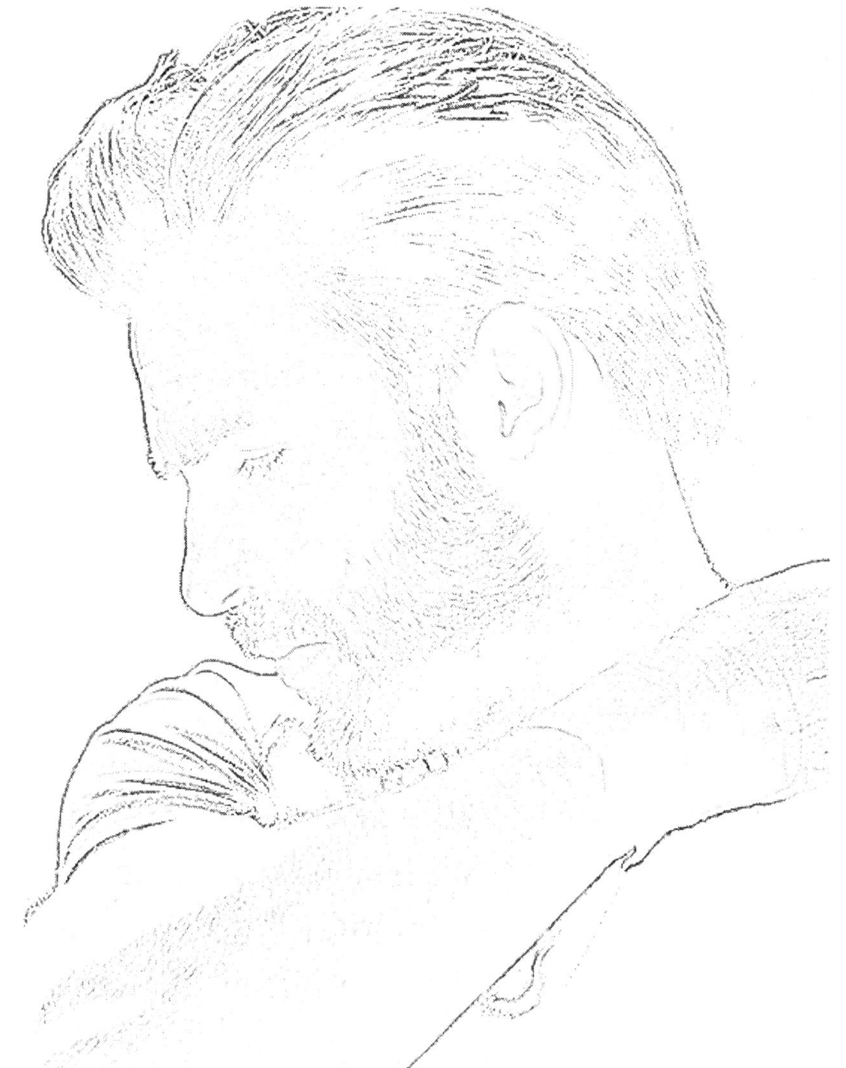

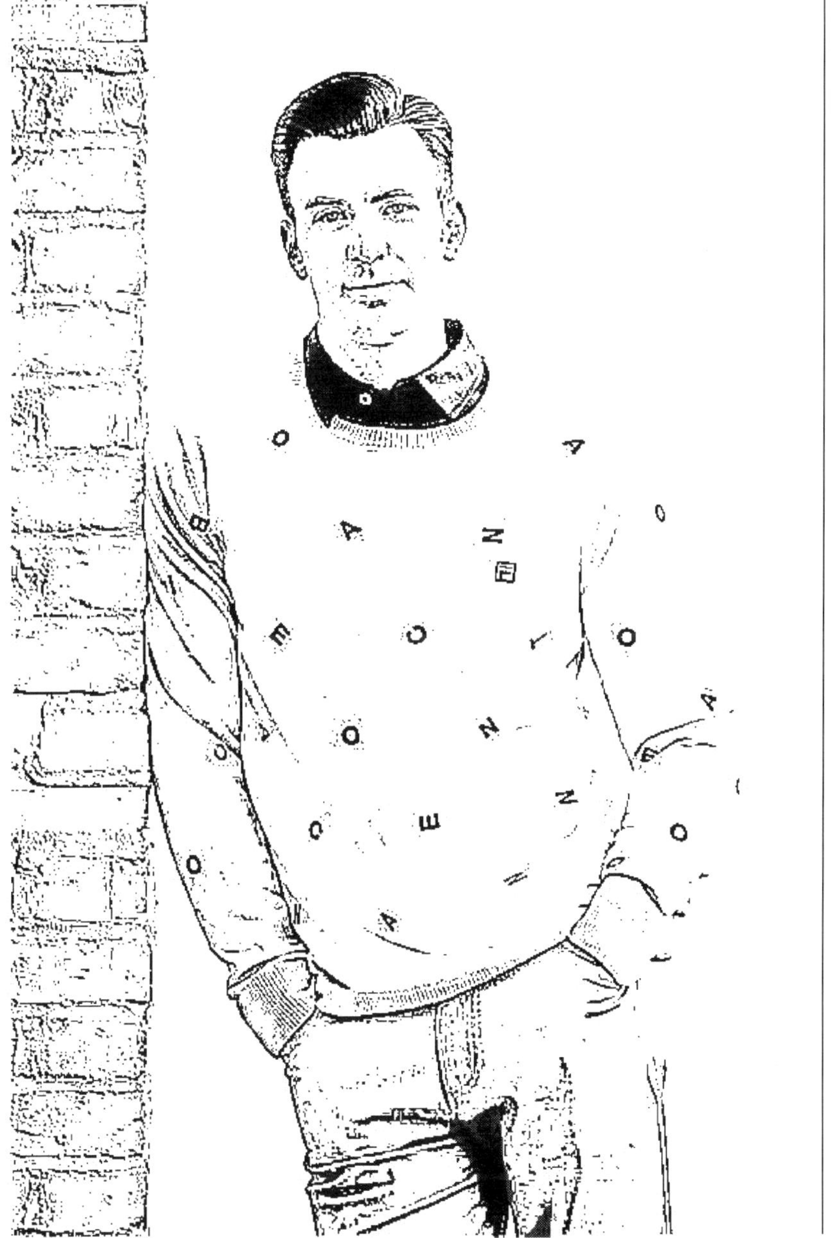

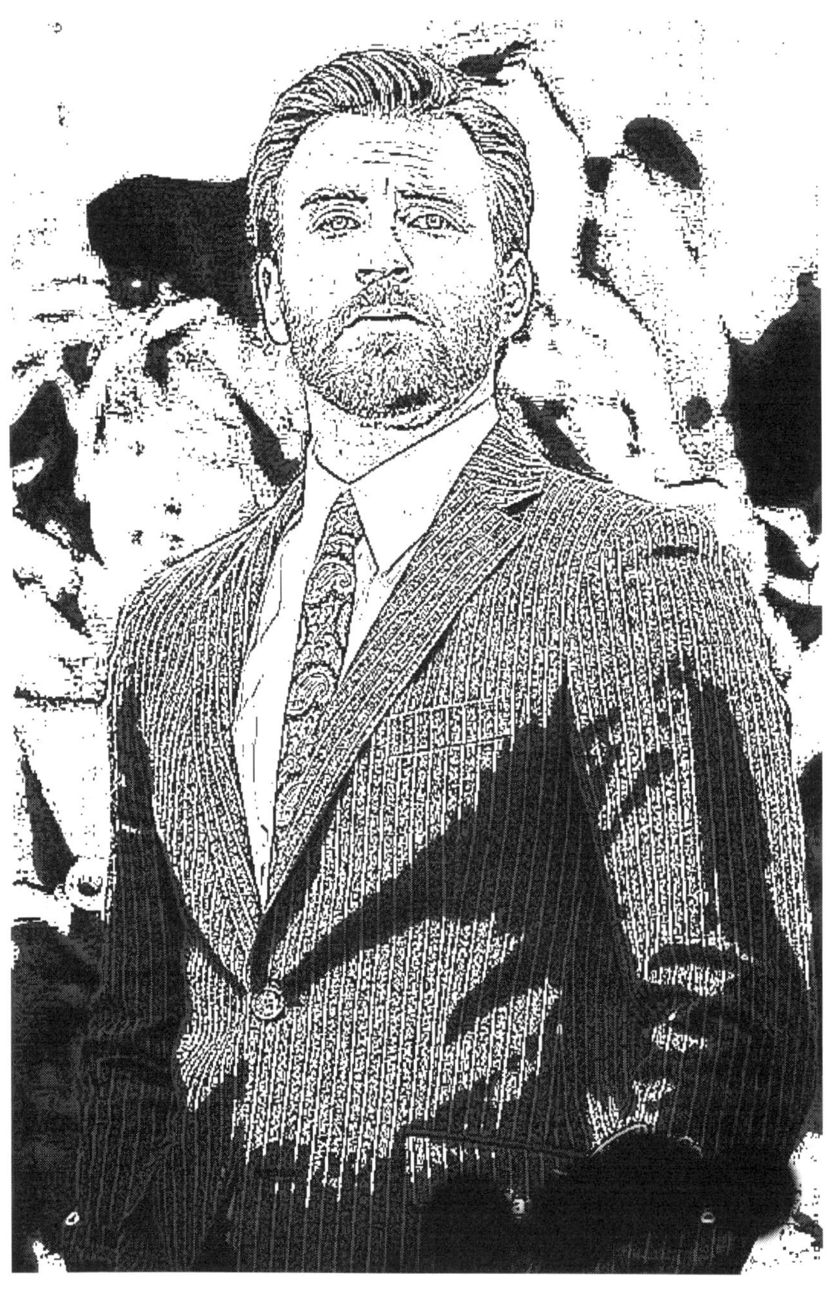

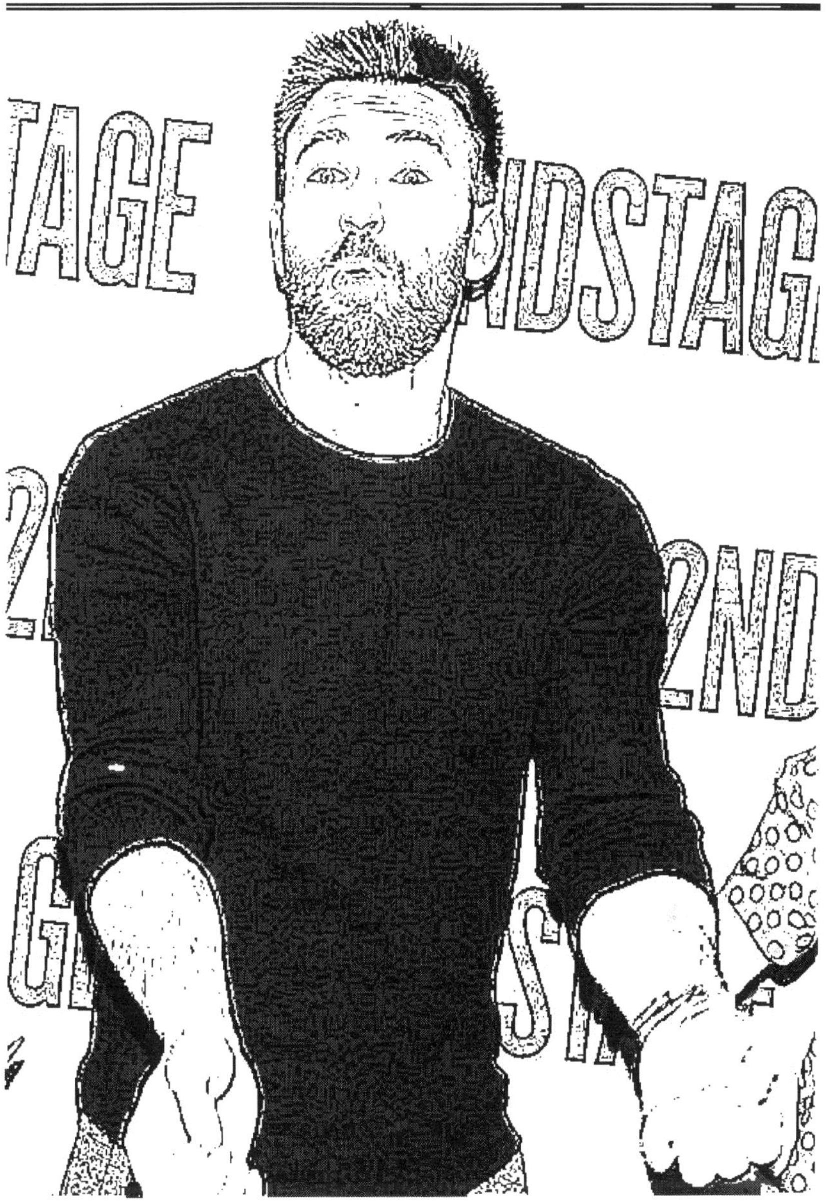

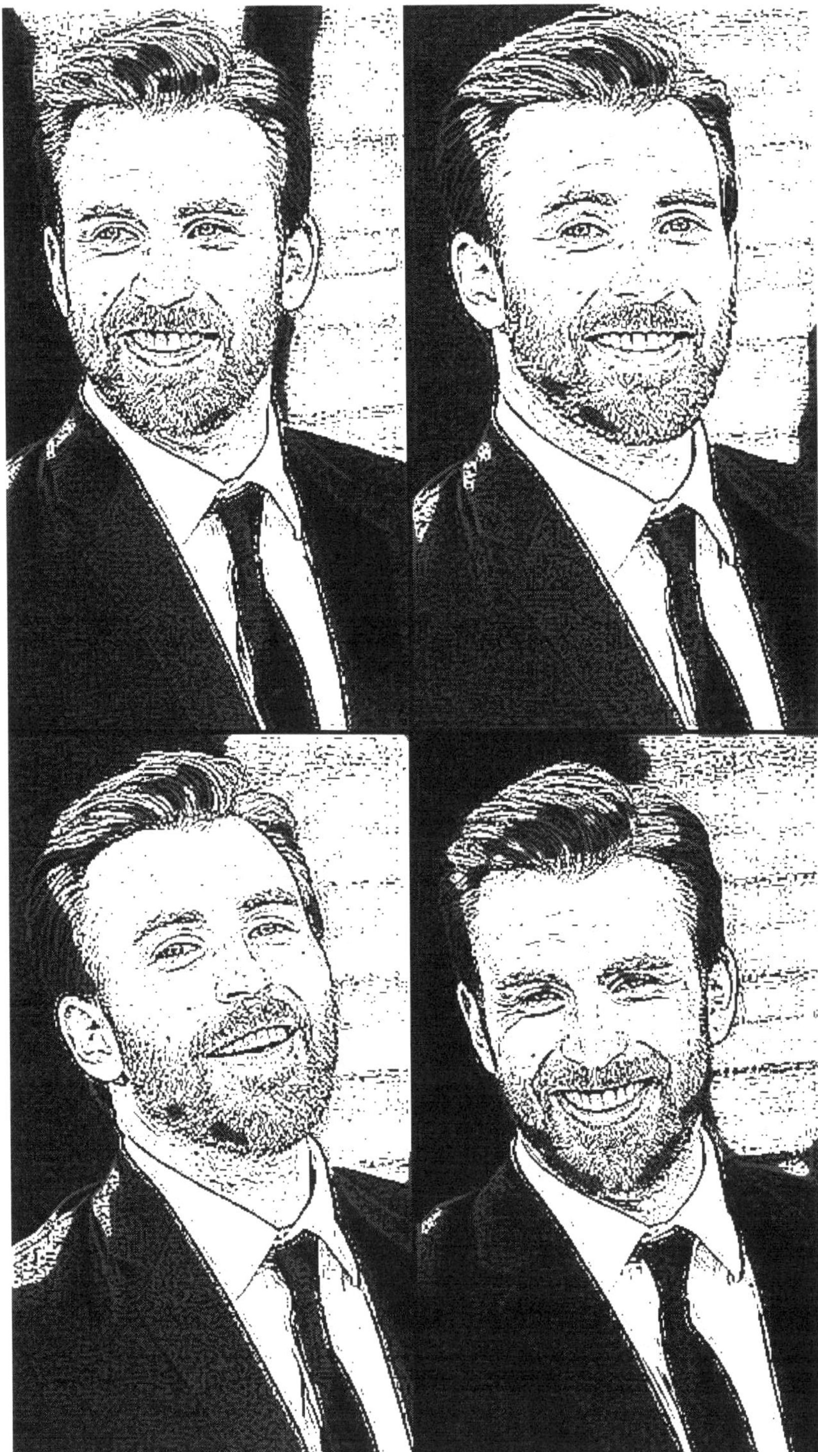

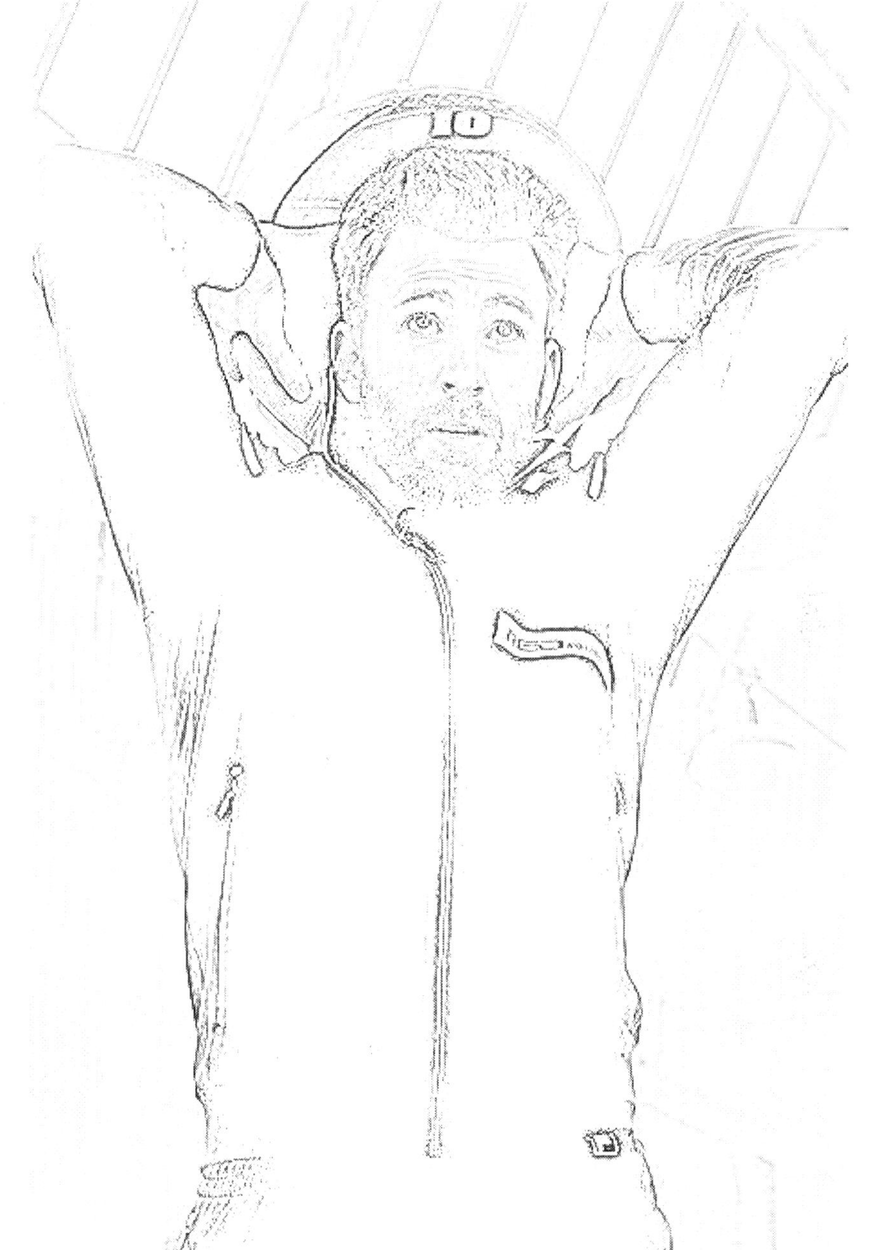

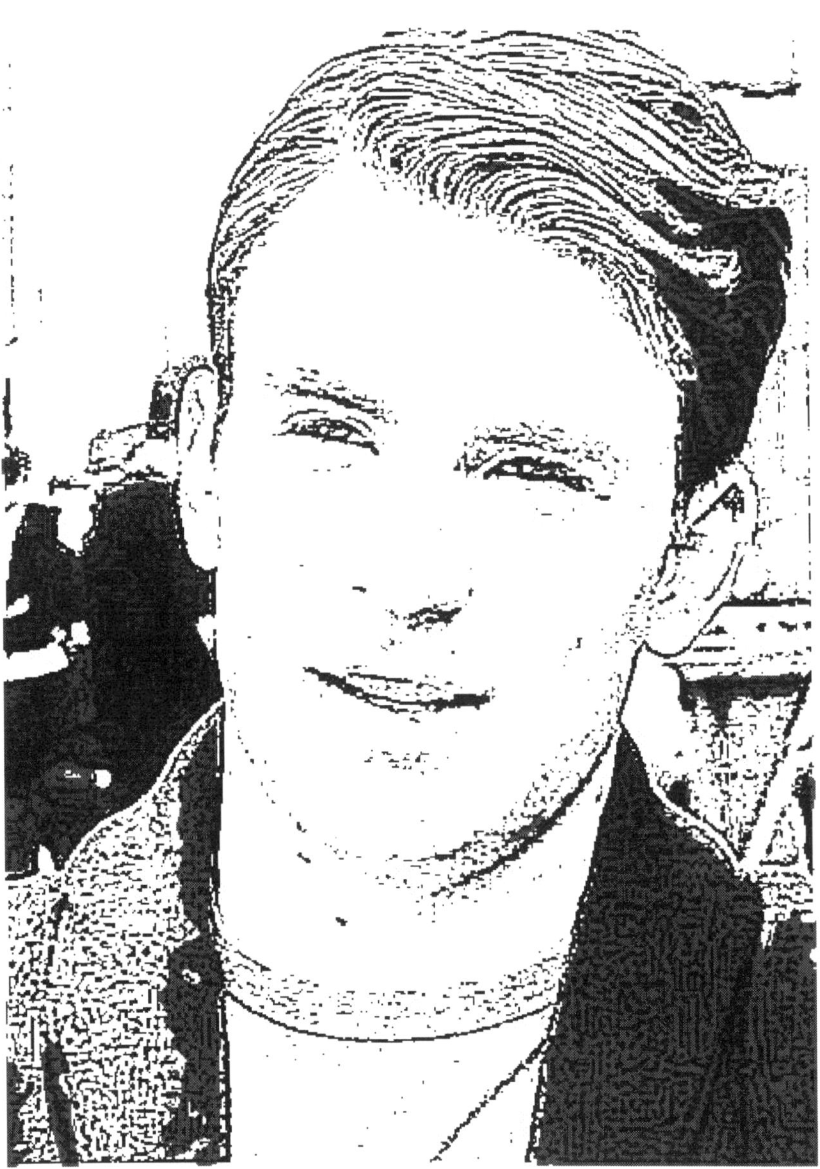

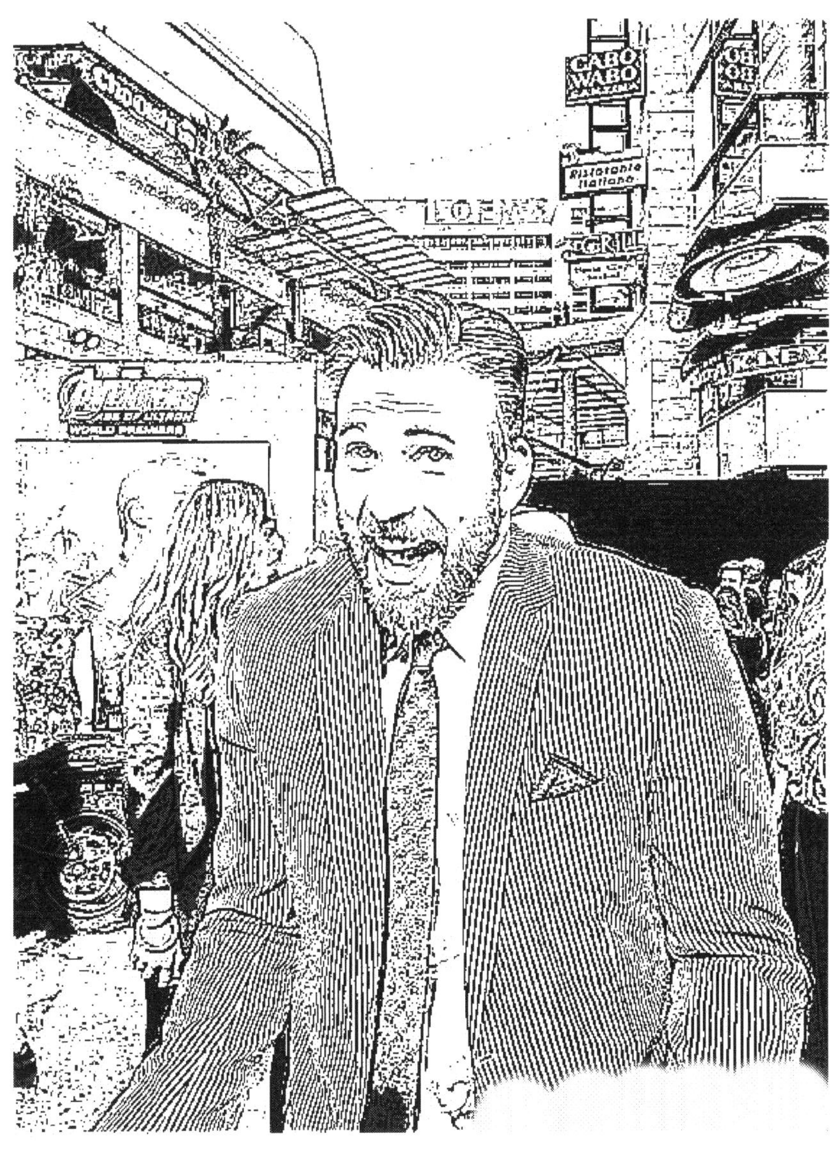
LOEWS
CABO WABO
Ristorante Italiano
GRILL

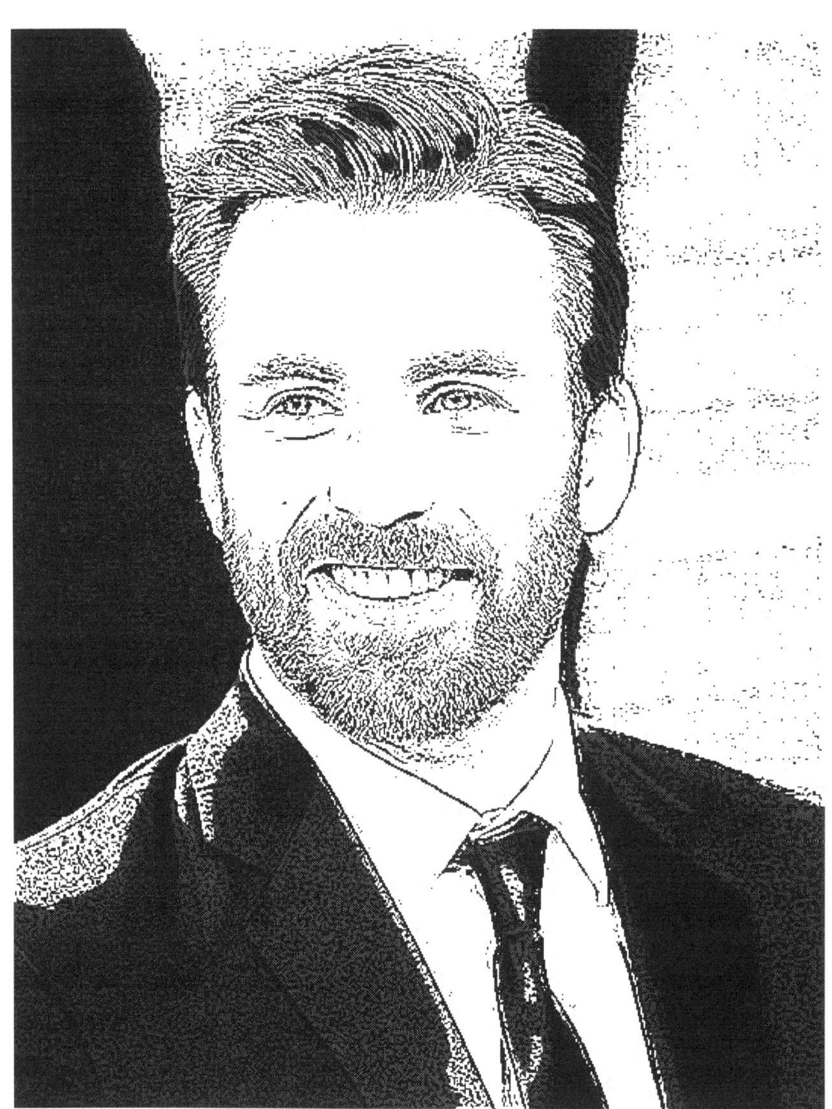

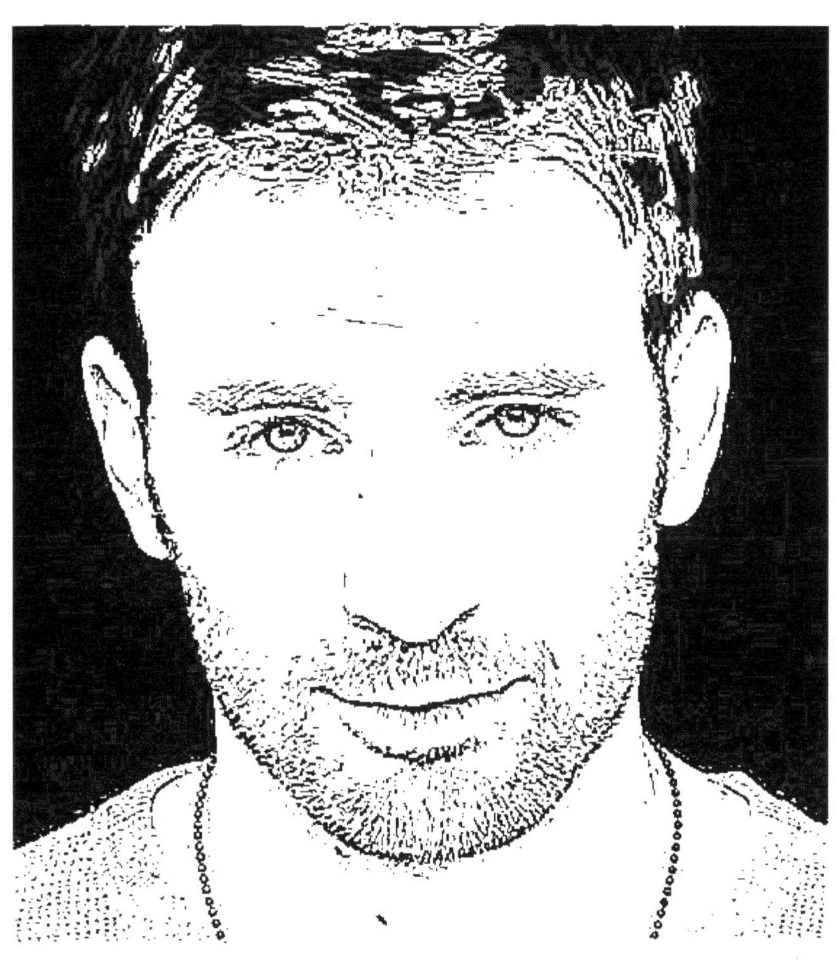

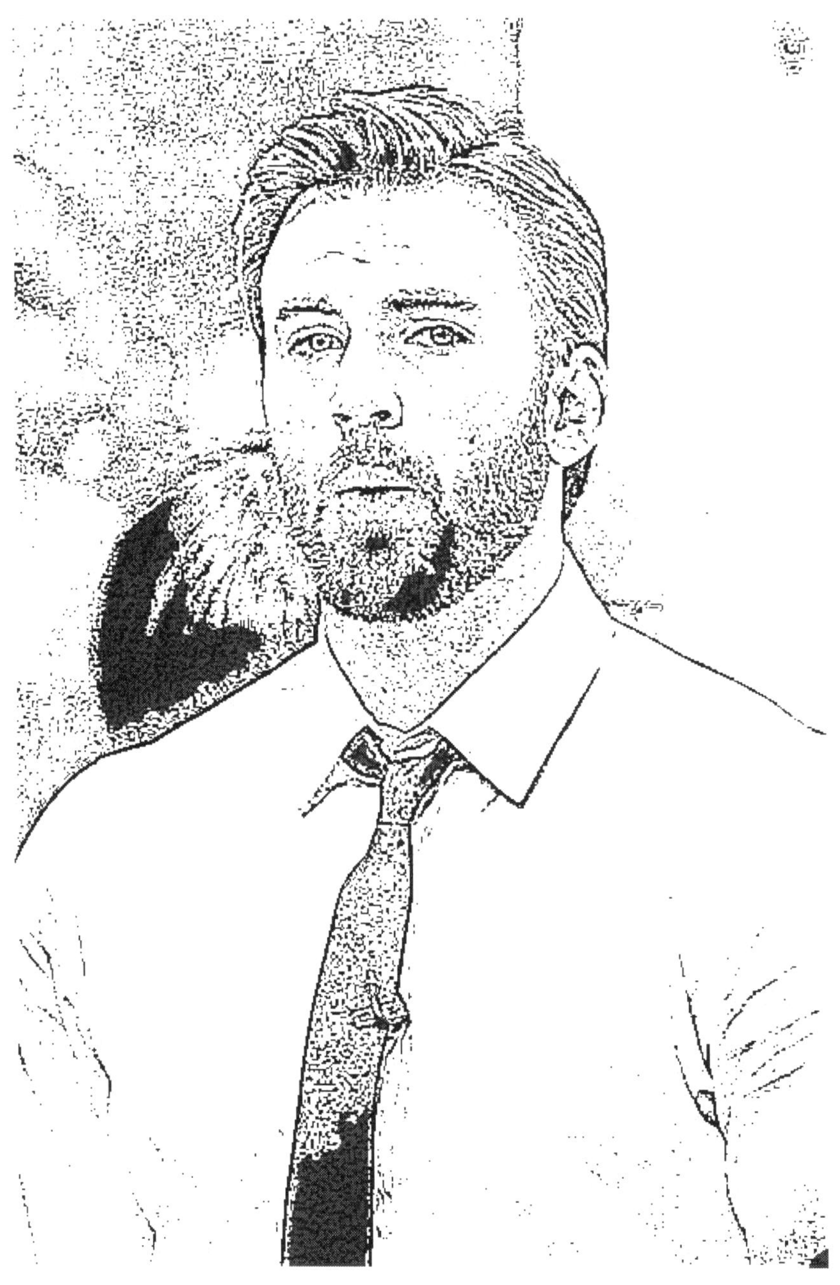

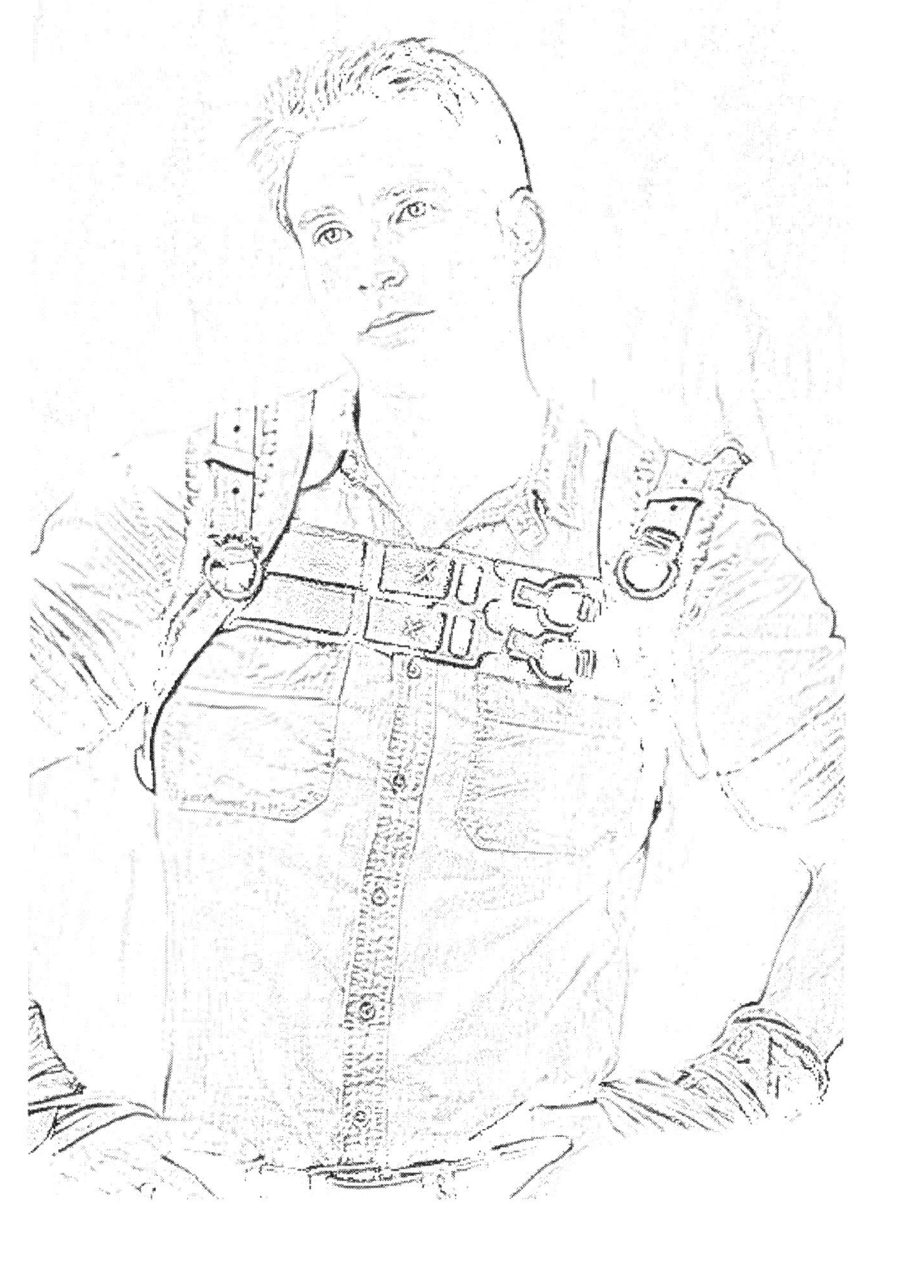

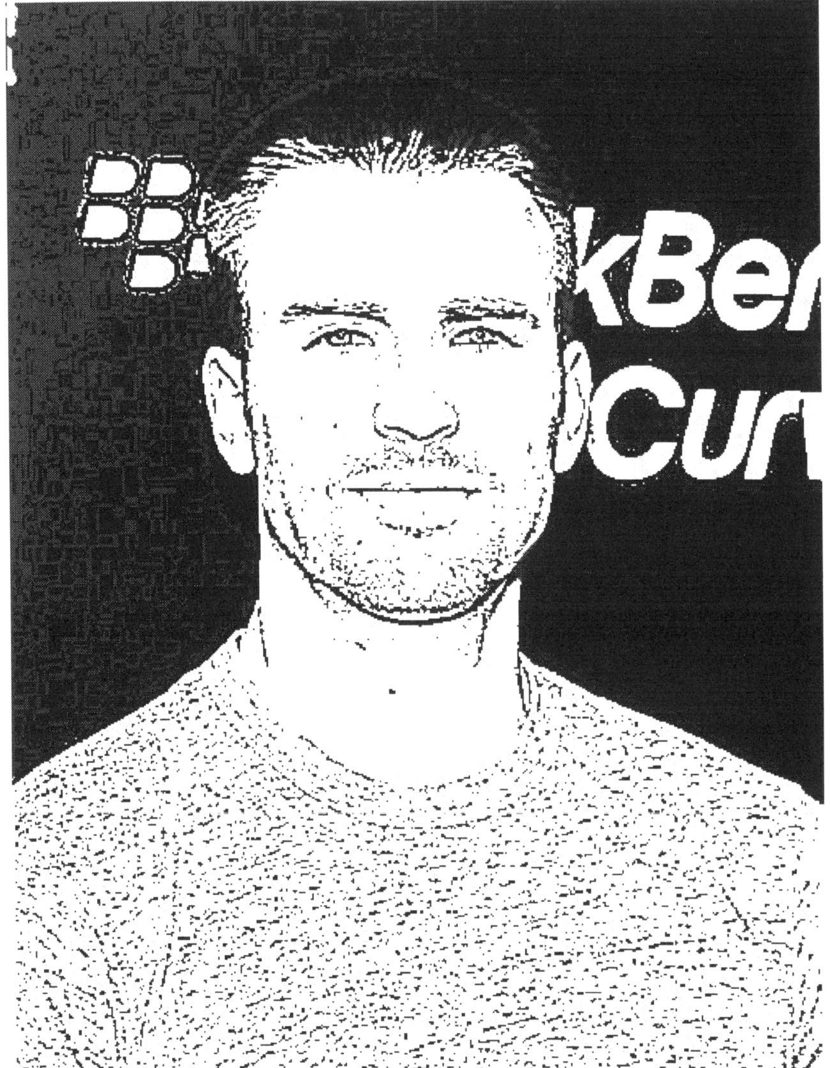

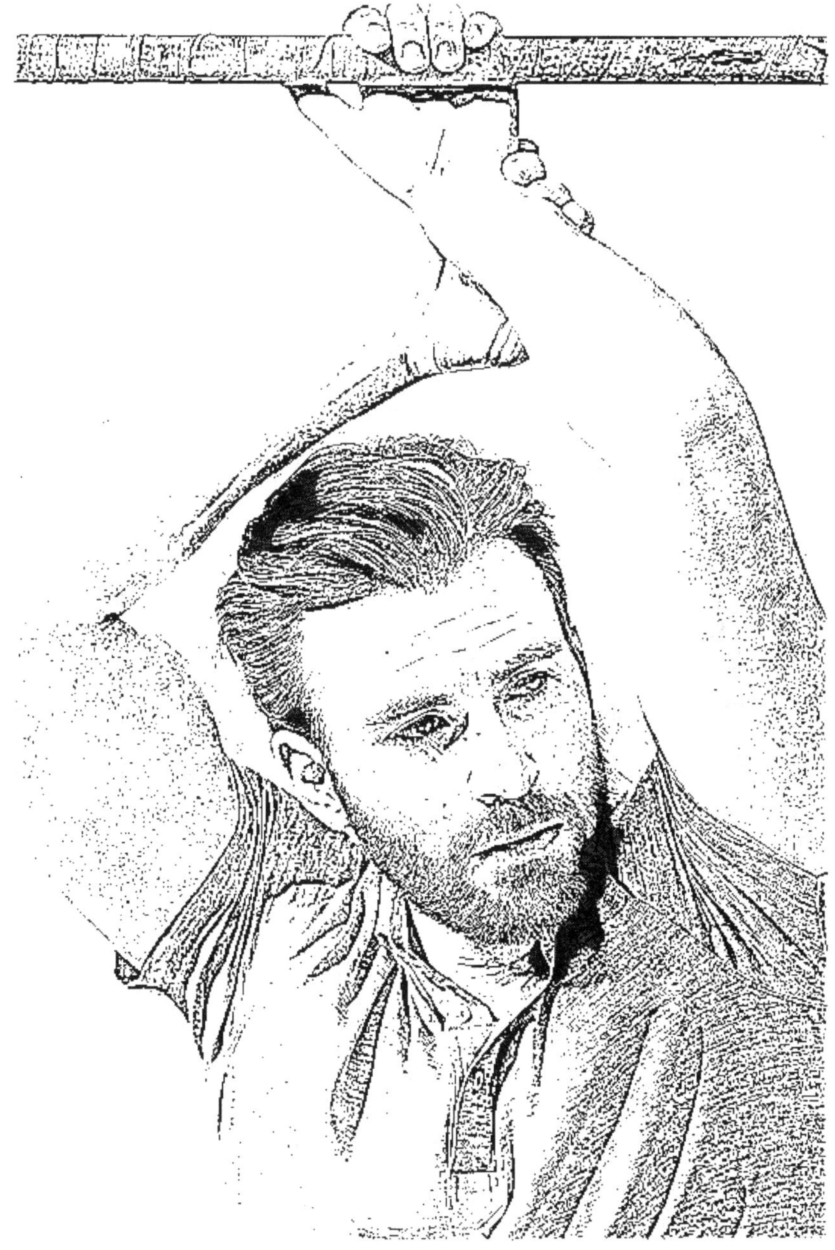

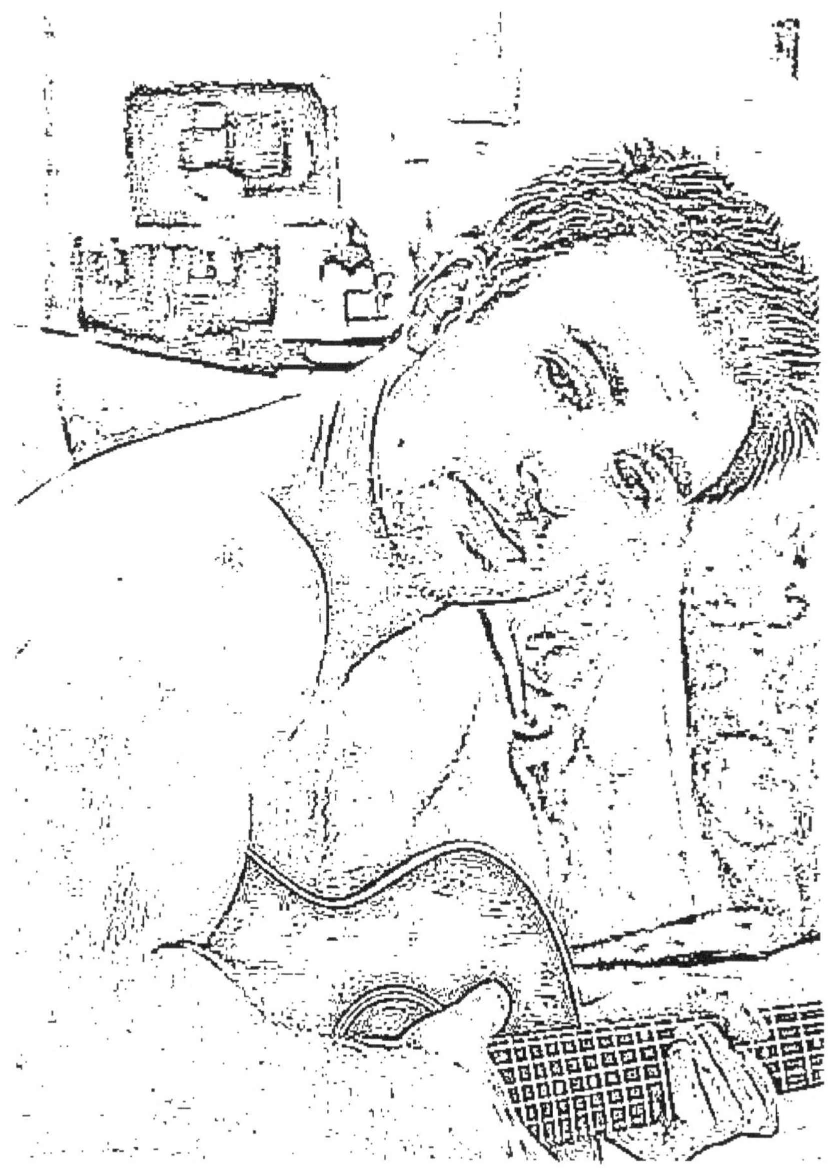

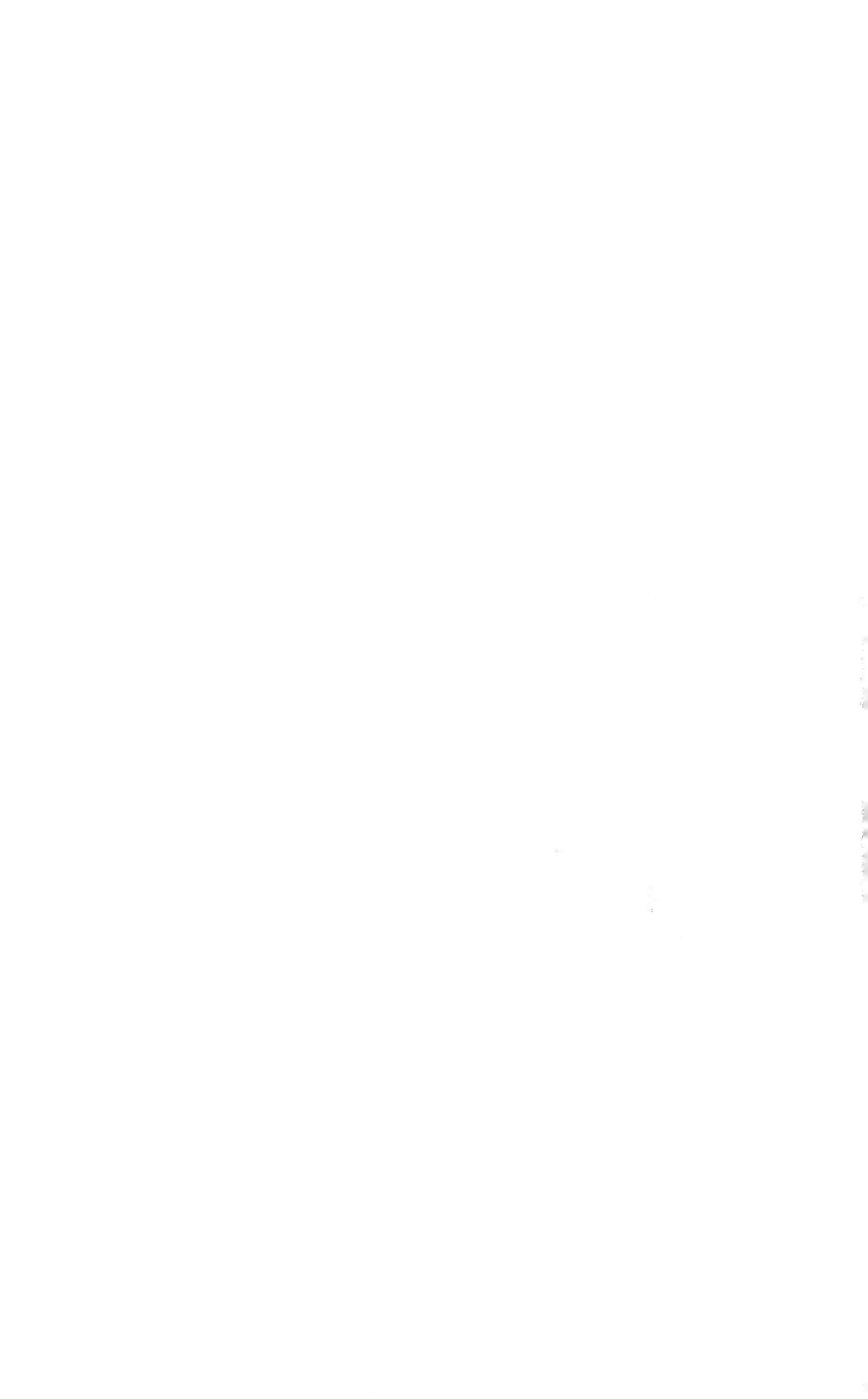

Made in the USA
Middletown, DE
17 September 2020

19965733R00024